365 BADASS BLACK KID AFFIRMATIONS

POSITIVE THOUGHTS FOR GIRLS AND BOYS TO CREATE STRONG, HAPPY, CONFIDENT AND EMPOWERED CHILDREN AND YOUNG ADULTS

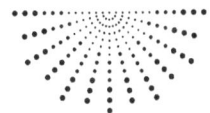

JASMINE GREENE

CONTENTS

INTRODUCTION

Hello. My name is Jasmine, and I am thrilled that you are here with me today. Being a kid is hard sometimes, and the world can occasionally tear us down, so together, we will discover how amazing you truly are. Over the next few chapters, we are going to feed your mind with powerful, positive thoughts. Your only job is to commit to reading this book every day, and in no time, you will become the best version of yourself. You deserve to accomplish anything and everything you put your mind to.

It's hard to predict what life is going to throw at you from day to day, so I've divided the affirmation into nine chapters. If you are struggling with one area in your life, it would be best to focus on this section. You are welcome to read the affirmations out loud or in your head. When you have finished reading for the day, pick one affirmation that made you feel great and repeat it throughout the day.

Buckle up and get ready for this crazy journey. I will see you stronger, happier, and a little bit older on the other side.

RISE AND SHINE

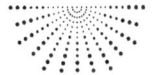

1. I'm going to have a good day.

2. I wake up each morning with a smile.

3. Today is a fresh start.

4. I am ready for this day.

5. I am well rested.

6. Today is going to be my day.

7. I will be a good listener today.

8. I can be anything I want to be

9. I am in control of my emotions.

10. Today I will spread positivity.

11. I'm choosing to have an amazing day.

12. Today I am a leader.

13. I have everything I need to succeed today.

14. Today I am going to shine.

15. I am energized.

16. Today is a new beginning.

17. I feel healthy and strong today.

18. I am happy and content with my life.

19. I have everything I need to make today a great day.

20. I am resilient.

21. I'm going to make today count.

22. Today I will work through my fears.

23. Every day and in every way, I get better and better.

24. All is well in the world.

25. I woke up today feeling empowered.

26. Today, I will be present in the moment.

27. I feel awake and alert.

28. Today I choose to think positive.

29. I can accomplish anything today.

30. I woke up today for a purpose.

31. I choose my own attitude every day.

32. Today I will be confident.

33. Today will be great.

34. I am excited for this day.

35. Today is the perfect day to be happy.

36. Every day brings new opportunities.

37. Thank you for this new day.

38. I'm starting a new chapter today.

2
I CAN DO ANYTHING

1. I have great ideas.

2. I'm going to take a chance.

3. My confidence grows when I step outside of my comfort zone.

4. I have faith in myself.

5. I stand up for my beliefs.

6. I have many unique gifts and talents.

7. I am brave.

8. With every breath, I feel stronger.

9. I can do hard things.

10. I am capable.

11. I stand up for things I believe in.

12. I am courageous even when things are unknown to me.

13. I am exactly where I need to be.

14. I embrace change.

15. I am confident.

16. I listen to my inner wisdom.

17. I can handle this.

18. I have the courage to be myself.

19. My choices are my own.

20. I have everything I need.

21. I am exactly where I need to be.

22. My confidence increases every day.

23. No matter how hard it is, I can do it.

24. I trust myself.

25. I am awesome.

26. I know challenges offer an opportunity to grow.

27. I can make good choices.

28. I believe in myself.

29. I can totally do this.

30. I am a hard worker.

31. I can be a leader.

32. I have the words I need to express myself.

33. I stand up for myself.

34. I am not afraid to tackle big things.

35. I can say no.

36. I will get through this.

37. I can do anything.

38. I am strong and determined.

39. I have courage in everything that I do.

40. I can do whatever I focus my mind on.

41. I can achieve my dreams.

42. I can and I will.

43. Being true to myself is what matters.

3
LEARNING & EDUCATION

1. My brain is powerful.

2. I love to solve problems!

3. I am smart.

4. I don't know everything and that is ok!

5. I express my ideas easily.

6. Doing my best is enough.

7. Every problem has an answer.

8. I am capable.

9. I am open to new ideas.

10. I am always learning.

11. I can do anything I put my mind to.

12. I work hard.

13. Changing my mind is a strength, not a weakness

14. I am open and ready to learn.

15. I trust my intuition.

16. I enjoy absorbing knowledge.

17. I am intelligent.

18. I manage my time well.

19. I trust in my ability to solve problems.

20. I like being punctual.

21. I am creative.

22. It's okay to not know everything.

23. I think before I react.

24. I can ask for help when I need it.

25. Learning is fun and exciting.

26. Sometimes I make mistakes but I choose to learn from them.

27. I complete my school work on time every day.

28. I give myself permission to make mistakes.

29. I strive to do my best every day.

30. I'm prepared to succeed.

31. I listen to my intuition.

32. I handle all my responsibilities and tasks well.

33. I am capable of so much.

34. I am expanding my mind every day.

35. The more I learn the more I will grow.

36. I am a great listener.

37. I always act responsibly.

4
GOOD VIBRATIONS

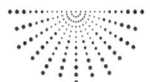

1. I choose to feel happy.

2. I radiate positive energy.

3. I deserve all good things.

4. My positive thoughts create positive feelings.

5. Wonderful and awesome things happen to me.

6. I am always in the right place at the right time.

7. Good things are going to come to me.

8. I enjoy discovering something new.

9. I can experience beauty wherever I go.

10. My happiness is up to me.

11. I see the good in myself.

12. I am a positive influence.

13. I am a good sport.

14. I deserve happiness.

15. I choose to think positive.

16. Bad emotions will pass.

17. I spread joy.

18. I have good ideas.

19. There is joy in my life.

20. There is always a reason to smile.

21. Happy thoughts create happy feelings.

22. I try to look on the bright side.

23. I find the fun in life.

24. I enjoy being happy.

25. There's no such thing as a wrong emotion.

26. I am calm and relaxed.

27. I have loving, positive, and happy thoughts.

28. I start with a positive mindset.

29. I am caring.

30. I celebrate my accomplishments.

31. I surround myself with positive people.

32. I look for opportunities to laugh.

33. I am joyful.

34. Wonderful things are going to happen to me.

35. I can control my own happiness.

36. I choose my attitude.

37. I show the world my beautiful smile.

38. I am thoughtful and kind.

39. I am a good friend to myself.

40. I let my light shine.

5
ALWAYS BE GRATEFUL

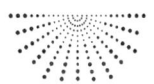

1. Today, I am grateful.

2. I will take deep breaths.

3. I am thankful for everything in my life.

4. I am grateful for another day to grow on my journey.

5. I am proud of myself.

6. My life is beautiful.

7. I appreciate the good things in my life.

8. I am grateful for all I have.

9. God has blessing me with an amazing family.

10. I am grateful to be exactly where I am.

11. I am thankful for being who I am.

12. I am so grateful to be alive.

13. I am grateful for my black body

14. I am thankful for my blessings.

15. I am loving.

16. I am filled with gratitude.

17. I am thankful for my parent's sacrifices.

18. Today and every day, I am blessed.

19. I am grateful for all the people in my life

20. I have everything I need right now.

21. I am a magnet for blessings.

22. I am thankful for today.

23. I am grateful for who I am.

24. I can live in the moment.

25. I invite gratitude into my heart

26. I am grateful for everything my family has done for me.

27. I love that I love what I love.

FAMILY & RELATIONSHIPS

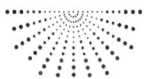

1. I respect others.

2. I always obey my parent's instructions.

3. I can see love and affection in the eyes of my family members.

4. I am friendly.

5. My parents will always take care of my needs.

6. I bring out the good in others.

7. My parents' support allows me to achieve anything in life.

8. I like to help my family.

9. My family is always there to help me.

10. I am surrounded by love.

11. I am protected.

12. I care about others.

13. I will never abandon my family.

14. I do not wish for anything except safety and security for my family members.

15. I can talk about and share my feelings.

16. I will never say NO to any reasonable demands from my family members.

17. We all take care of each other's needs.

18. I am helpful.

19. My family members never fail to make me happy.

20. I will make time for my family.

21. I am my family's strength.

22. I share an unconditional love for them.

23. I am forgiving.

24. I trust my family members with everything.

25. I accept compliments from others.

26. I will treat others the way I want to be treated.

27. I am an important part of my family.

28. I am only in control of my own actions. I cannot control others.

29. I get inspiration from my family.

30. I am never alone.

31. I will always make sure that my family is doing okay.

32. I support others with love and kindness.

33. I try to see the good in others.

34. I am one of the reasons my family is happy.

35. I will never let my family down because of my behavior.

36. I am considerate of other people's feelings.

37. I make like-minded friends easily and naturally.

38. I am a good friend.

39. I receive love from my family.

40. I have people who love and respect me.

41. I don't try to tear down other people.

42. I am a wonderful friend.

43. I include others.

44. My family has my best interest in mind.

45. I make other people feel better.

46. I always share.

47. I treat others with compassion.

48. I do not have to keep secrets from my family members because I know they will understand.

49. I am honored to have a family like mine.

50. I will take care of my family.

51. I am generous.

52. I have no harsh emotions for anyone.

53. I am comfortable communicating with my family members.

54. I give daily love to all the members in my family.

55. My family loves me so much!

56. I will respect other peoples boundaries and I will tell others to respect mine.

57. I am happy when they are happy.

58. I take my family's criticisms positively.

59. I will respect all the emotions in my family.

60. I am everyone's friend.

61. I can forgive others.

62. I love my family and friends.

63. I let my family have their personal space.

64. I am an asset to my community.

65. I love to watch my family doing well.

66. I am gentle with myself and others.

67. My family is always there for one another.

7
I AM AMAZING

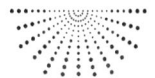

1. I like myself.

2. I am perfect just the way I am.

3. I am extraordinary.

4. I listen to my body.

5. I enjoy spending time with myself.

6. I am beautiful inside and out.

7. I am enough.

8. I am a good person

9. My differences make me special.

10. My black body is beautiful.

11. I am honest and trustworthy.

12. My possibilities are endless.

13. I am becoming the best version of myself.

14. I am proud of who I am.

15. My hair is the perfect halo for my head.

16. My voice is powerful.

17. I love myself.

18. My skin is gorgeous.

19. I have inner beauty.

20. I am important.

21. I am whole and complete.

22. I am worthy of love.

23. I am healthy and am growing up well.

24. My body is beautifully perfect.

25. There is no one better to be than myself.

26. I get better every single day.

27. I am truthful.

28. I am an amazing person.

29. I deserve to be loved.

30. I try to be the best version of myself.

31. I believe in myself and my abilities.

32. I matter.

33. I don't want to look like anyone but myself.

34. I won't compare myself to others. Everyone is on their own path.

35. I am strong inside and out.

36. I am whole.

37. I accept myself for who I am.

38. I don't need to be perfect.

39. I am beautiful.

40. I strive for progress, not perfection.

41. I am an original.

42. I deeply love and accept myself.

43. I am unique and special.

44. My weirdness is wonderful.

45. I only compare myself to myself.

46. I am valuable.

8

NEVER GIVE UP

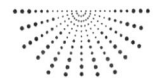

1. It's okay to make mistakes.

2. I get better every single day

3. I don't give up after failing once.

4. I have a lot to be proud of.

5. Failure helps me learn.

6. I forgive others for their mistakes.

7. I am working on myself.

8. I forgive myself for making a mistake.

9. I believe in myself.

10. The more I let it go, the better I will feel.

11. I replace anger with compassion.

12. I will be okay.

13. It's okay if I don't have the answers.

14. I understand how to apologize when I need to.

15. I can learn from my mistakes.

16. All of my problems have solutions.

17. My mistakes help me learn and grow.

18. My challenges help me grow.

19. I can get through anything.

20. I get better and better every day.

21. Anything is possible.

22. My success is just around the corner.

23. I'm going to push through.

24. I've got this.

25. It's okay to be scared.

26. Everything will be okay.

27. I can take it one step at a time.

28. I'm working at my own pace.

29. I am going to get through this.

30. My feelings are important.

31. I believe anything is possible.

32. I accomplish great results.

33. I turn failures into opportunities for success.

34. Mistakes are how I grow

35. I am free to make my own choices.

36. I am going to get through this.

37. I have inner strength.

38. I am worthy.

39. I welcome new experiences.

40. I am persistent.

41. Challenges help me become a stronger person.

42. I will do better next time.

43. I have so much potential.

44. Trust can be earned.

45. I believe in me.

46. I like to keep trying, even when things are hard.

47. I am always moving forward.

48. I am optimistic.

49. I believe in myself and my abilities.

50. Problems challenge me to better myself.

51. I embrace my fears fully and calmly.

52. I am in charge of my life.

53. I am deserving of love, trust, and kindness.

54. I can be anything I want to be.

55. I trust myself to make great decisions.

9

MY FUTURE IS BRIGHT

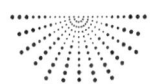

1. I am open to possibility.

2. I trust my decisions.

3. I am patient.

4. I can get better at things if I practice.

5. I enjoy letting events unfold in good time.

6. I believe I can be whatever I want to be.

7. I have a beautiful imagination.

8. I believe in my dreams.

9. I can make a difference.

10. I am building my future.

11. I am changing every day.

12. I am true to my word.

13. Small steps move me forward.

14. My life matters.

15. I have a strong and important voice.

16. I can change the world.

17. My future is my own.

18. I can become whatever I want to be.

19. I choose to look for the best way forward for myself.

20. I enjoy challenging myself with new ideas and possibilities.

21. I give myself permission to make choices.

22. I am a product of my decisions.

23. I am strong and determined.

24. I can make a difference.

25. I am the only me in the whole world.

26. I can adapt to anything.

27. I have many talents.

28. I play an important role in the world.

29. I am my own person.

30. I matter.

31. I belong here.

32. I will use my voice

33. There is room for me at the table

34. My words have power. I will use them wisely.

35. I am a good influence on others.

36. I radiate love and compassion.

37. I will make a difference.

38. I can make my dreams come true.

39. I stand up for what I believe in.

40. I am making the right choices.

41. I decide my own attitude.

42. I make my own choices.

43. I think for myself.

44. I make the world a better place.

45. I believe in my goals and dreams.

46. Whatever I do, I give it my best.

47. Every day brings new opportunities.

48. I have the power to make my dreams true.

CONCLUSION

Congratulations! You are now on your way to becoming a strong and successful adult. If you feel like this book helped you, it would be fantastic if you could leave a review on Amazon. Reviews will help this book reach other black kids that need to be told they are amazing and powerful too. Let's get this book out there to as many kids as we can and make this world full of powerful children. Just imagine if all black kids knew their true worth! Ah, what a pretty picture!

BONUS #1: AFFIRMATIONS FOR SIBLINGS

1. I am a leader, my siblings look up to me.

2. I realize that sometimes we will fight and that is ok.

3. My siblings can count on me.

4. Our relationship is getting stronger every day.

5. I show I care with love.

6. When we are grown, I will remain close to my siblings.

7. I feel good when my siblings thrive.

8. I am so happy that I have siblings.

9. I want the best for siblings but never judge.

10. I love and accept my siblings.

11. Each special occasion brings us closer together.

12. Change is okay.

13. I receive positive energy from my siblings.

14. I love spending time with my siblings.

15. I am special.

16. I maintain peace and calm when speaking to my siblings.

17. I play an important role in the family.

18. My siblings and I are close.

19. My mom and dad love me for who I am!

20. Each of my siblings have different strengths and that is ok.

21. I am setting a great example for my siblings.

22. My siblings are my support system and I am theirs.

23. Our relationship gets stronger every day.

24. I am not a reflection of my siblings' actions.

25. I am always there for my siblings, we laugh and cry together.

26. Every day I give thanks for my wonderful family.

27. My siblings and I are all special.

28. I love my siblings!

29. I do not need to take responsibility for my siblings' actions.

30. My siblings consider my feelings and respect my privacy.

31. My siblings and I love spending time together.

32. I have many unique talents.

33. I am lucky because I have amazing siblings.

34. My siblings and I support one another.

35. My siblings are some of the most positive parts of my life.

36. My siblings will alway be there for me when I need help.

37. My siblings all have unique talents.

38. Thank you for blessing me with such amazing siblings.

39. I try to be a good role model for my siblings.

40. I am helpful.

41. We love, respect and appreciate each other.

42. I am truly worthy of a great relationship with my siblings.

43. When my siblings are not feeling well, I let them know I care.

44. We are all on this path together.

BONUS #2: AFFIRMATIONS FOR CHILDREN WITH A BROTHER

1. I love and accept my brother as he is.

2. I will always be a best friend to my brother.

3. My brother is always there for me whenever I need help.

4. Because I have a brother, I will always have a friend.

5. My brother expressed love to me in the best way he knows how.

6. I love my brother and he is simply amazing.

7. Having a brother means being there for each other.

8. I am so grateful to have such a wonderful brother in my life.

9. My brother and I grow closer everyday.

10. I know my brother will always be there for me.

11. I am proud to be my brother's sibling.

12. I believe that my brother will do great things.

13. I always show my brother kindness.

14. I realize that sometimes we will fight and that is ok.

15. I am very lucky to have a brother.

16. My brother never fails to make me happy.

17. My brother and I support one another.

18. I maintain peace and calm when speaking to my brother.

19. My brother can count on me.

20. I feel good when my brother thrives.

21. I like spending time with my brother.

22. I am grateful for my brother everyday.

BONUS #3: AFFIRMATIONS FOR CHILDREN WITH A SISTER

1. I love and accept my sister as she is.

2. I will always be a best friend to my sister.

3. My sister is always there for me whenever I need help.

4. Because I have a sister I will always have a friend.

5. My sister expressed love to me in the best way she knows how.

6. I love my sister and she is simply amazing.

7. Having a sister means being there for each other.

8. I am so grateful to have such a wonderful sister in my life.

9. My sister and I grow closer everyday.

10. I know my sister will always be there for me.

11. I am proud to be my sister' sibling.

12. I believe that my sister will do great things.

13. I always show my sister kindness.

14. I realize that sometimes we will fight and that is ok.

15. I am very lucky to have a sister.

16. My sister never fails to make me happy.

17. My sister and I support one another.

18. I maintain peace and calm when speaking to my sister.

19. My sister can count on me.

20. I feel good when my sister thrives.

21. I like spending time with my sister.

22. I am grateful for my sister everyday.

REFERENCES

Hall, L. (2021, May 19). *101+ Positive Affirmations for Kids to Boost Confidence and Self-Esteem.* Self-Sufficient Kids. https://selfsufficientkids.com/affirmations-for-kids/

LaScala, M. (2021, February 5). *100 Positive Affirmations for Kids, From Toddlers to Teens.* Good Housekeeping. https://www.goodhousekeeping.com/life/parenting/g35309300/best-affirmations-for-kids/?slide=100

mindbodygreen. (2021, January 21). *A Master List Of 50+ Affirmations To Make Mornings Infinitely Brighter.* https://www.mindbodygreen.com/articles/morning-affirmations

P. (2021a, June 6). *101 Positive Affirmations for Kids.* The Pathway 2 Success. https://www.

thepathway2success.com/101-positive-affirmations-for-kids/

P. (2021b, June 10). *105 powerful morning affirmations for a good day*. Kids n Clicks. https://kidsnclicks.com/morning-affirmations/

S. (2021c, April 2). *Affirmations For Kids: How to Empower Your Child*. Mightier. https://www.mightier.com/articles/affirmations-for-kids/

www.ingramcontent.com/pod-product-compliance
Lightning Source LLC
Chambersburg PA
CBHW061325120626
46546CB00007B/2681